Wisdom for Fathers

Boyd Bailey

Cover designed by truth in advertising
© 2014 Wisdom Hunters, LLC
Published by Wisdom Hunters, LLC
http://www.wisdomhunters.com
Book ISBN: 978-0615827148

INTRODUCTION

How do you feel as a father? Inadequate at times? Overwhelmed most of the time? Yet, the fulfillment of being a father cannot be properly put into words without experiencing its raw reality. No doubt, struggles in fatherhood are an opportunity to approach your heavenly Father in humble dependence in need of wisdom, faith, and encouragement. God the Father's character is the example for earthly fathers to aspire to.

It's more difficult to grow as a father if, while you were growing up, your own father was absent or unengaged in your life. This cannot become an excuse for bad fathering, but it can be a point to address past pain. Without the medicinal application of forgiveness to a hurting heart and emotional wholeness from grace, there remains a hole in the heart."He heals the brokenhearted and binds up their wounds" (Psalm 147:3).

Dads who have not engaged in a spiritual, mental, and emotional process of inner healing express their pain in outward frustration, anger, and even depression. For fathers to father well, they must be fathered well. Praise the Lord if your father on earth accurately represents your Father in heaven. If not, you can appeal straight to heaven and receive God's healing power. Wise fathers process past pain, so their heart is healthy to love well.

Through Christ you can break the bondage of unfaithful fathering. Humility is the key, because it channels a man's strength into service and it molds his power into patience. A spirit-filled father is first concerned for his wife and children and places his own needs on the shelf of unselfishness for a season. Faithful fathers look out for their family first and defer their desires to later. Dads earn respect through humble service in the home.

"Therefore if you have any encouragement from being united with Christ, if any comfort from his love, if any common sharing in the Spirit, if any tenderness and compassion, then make my joy complete by being like-minded, having the same love, being one in spirit and of one mind. Do nothing out of selfish ambition or vain conceit. Rather, in humility value others above yourselves, not looking to your own interests but each of you to the interests of the others" (Philippians 2:1-4).

After 29 years, I still struggle to make good grades in the school of fatherhood, but I am blessed to be surrounded by great examples who have gone before me. I get close enough to their lives to learn from their mistakes and embrace their successes. Faithful ones can be found, but it takes intentionality to discover them. Once you find a fine father (you see it in the fruit from his wife and children), ask permission from him to pray and study together.

Seek first to be loved by your heavenly Father and learn from Him. Then engage earthly fathers who are worth following, and pour into other younger fathers who need you. Staying enrolled in the school of faithful fathering is both fun and frustrating. But with a heart guarded by and healed by your heavenly Father, it's the greatest job in the world.

OTHER BOOKS BY BOYD BAILEY

Seeking Daily the Heart of God, Volume I – a 365-day Devotional
Seeking Daily the Heart of God, Volume II – a 365-day Devotional
Infusion – a 90-day Devotional
Seeking God in the Psalms – a 90-day Devotional
Seeking God in the Proverbs – a 90-day Devotional
Wisdom for Marriage – a 30-day Devotional
Wisdom for Grads – a 30-day Devotional
Wisdom for Mothers – a 30-day Devotional
Wisdom for Work – a 30-day Devotional

JOIN OUR ONLINE COMMUNITY

SIGN UP for your free "Wisdom Hunters...Right Thinking" daily
devotional e-mail at **wisdomhunters.com**
"LIKE" us on Facebook at **facebook.com/wisdomhunters**
FOLLOW us on Twitter at **twitter.com/wisdomhunters**
SUBSCRIBE to us on YouTube at
youtube.com/wisdomhuntersvids
DOWNLOAD the free Wisdom Hunters App for
tablets and mobile devices on iTunes and Google Play

TABLE OF CONTENTS

1

Expecting A Baby

He [Joseph] went there to register with Mary, who was pledged to be married to him and was expecting a child. While they were there, the time came for the baby to be born, and she gave birth to her firstborn, a son. She wrapped him in cloths and placed him in a manger, because there was no room for them in the inn.
Luke 2:5-7

An expecting wife needs extra sensitivity and a strong, supportive husband. She is, at times, emotionally vulnerable and physically overwhelmed. As with Mary, there may be some uncertainty about the ultimate outcome, but she trusts the Lord to care for her and her baby. The circumstances are challenging when you are away from the comforts of home and its familiar feel. Pregnancy is a transition that requires trust in the Lord.

Husbands, your expecting wife needs you to step up like Joseph and provide leadership. This is not the time to lose faith or become frightened. Perfect love casts out fear, so overcome any apprehensions with the Christ-like love that dwells in your mind and heart. See pregnancy as a prayerful process to accomplish the plan of Almighty God, as expecting moms and dads can expect great things from Him. Hannah and her husband Elkanah gave God the glory for the blessing of their son Samuel:

"Early the next morning they arose and worshiped before the LORD and then went back to their home at Ramah. Elkanah made love to his wife Hannah, and the LORD remembered her. So in the course of time Hannah became pregnant and gave birth to a son. She named him Samuel, saying, 'Because I asked the LORD for him'" (1 Samuel 1:19-20).

A husband's leadership needs to provide protection for his wife. Accompany her, as Joseph did, to new places and people who might take advantage of your sweet-spirited spouse. It makes your woman feel safe and secure when you buffer her from bad people or strangers with unseemly motives. Stay with her, and see her through stressful situations, such as family members who can be awkward and insensitive toward your bride.

Intervene and defend your wife if your children, parents, or siblings show disrespect, regardless of how subtle it might be. God in marriage made you one flesh, so if she is offended, you are offended. Of course, prayerfully confront all parties in a spirit of grace and humility, but do so with clarity. An expecting wife is beautiful to behold, as she bears an innocent infant woven in her womb by God. Be there for her labor of love for the Lord and for His gift of a precious little one to love. Mary gave God the glory for her baby Jesus.

"The LORD has done this, and it is marvelous in our eyes" (Psalm 118:23).

Whom can I support and pray for who is expecting a baby? How can I thank m y heavenly Father for His gift of baby Jesus to mankind and me?

Related Readings: Isaiah 7:14; Micah 5:2; John 16:21; I John 4:18

2

Love Disciplines

He who spares the rod hates his son,
but he who loves him is careful to discipline him.
Proverbs 13:24

Love carefully disciplines; apathy silently ignores. Love looks for ways to instruct and improve, while busyness has no time for a tender touch of truth. Do you take the time to discipline your children? Do your offspring encounter your rebuke along with your encouragement? It is because we love them that we correct their attitudes and challenge them to better behavior. Rules restrain them from reacting foolishly or in the flesh.

How can our children learn to make wise decisions if we do not discipline them to love and obey God? Like warm lumps of clay in the hands of a skilled artist, our children are moldable; their character is pliable to be crafted by Christ. We seek consistency in our own character so that we have the moral authority and respect to lead them. Your child's first impression of the Lord is their father and mother, so be an authority that reveals His love.

The branch of a tree is easily bent when it is tender, so start when they are young in getting them to yield to Christ's Lordship. "Train a child in the way he should go, and when he is old he will not turn from it" (Proverbs 22:6). Foolishness flees from the faith and prayerful punishment of loving parents. "Folly is bound up in the heart of a child, but the rod of discipline will drive it far from him" (Proverbs 22:15). Discipline leads to freedom.

You may lament the need for respect from your son or daughter. It is your consistent concern for their character growth that invites their respect. "Fathers disciplined us and we respected them for it" (Hebrews 12:9). Loving parents honestly inquire, "Does my example of growth from my heavenly Father's discipline makes me an earthly father worth following?"

"For whom the LORD loves He reproves, Even as a father corrects the son in whom he delights" (Proverbs 3:12, NASB).

How do I respond to the Lord's discipline?

Related Readings: Proverbs 23:13-14; Proverbs 29:15-17; Hebrews 12:6-8; Ephesians 6:4

3

A Godly Legacy

When Jacob had finished giving instructions to his sons, he drew his feet up
into the bed, breathed his last and was gathered to his people.
Genesis 49:33

Jacob gave his dying instructions to his sons as they waited at his beside. They lingered there out of love and respect. They had observed his life. And though not perfect by far, it was a life of overall faithfulness to God. The sons of the father wanted to receive his blessing and they were proud of the legacy left to them, a legacy of faithfulness to God.

What legacy will you leave? If you died today, how would you be remembered? These are important questions for your children's sake. Maybe your parents did not leave you a godly heritage. Nevertheless, you have a wonderful opportunity to start a new tradition, one based on the principles of Scripture. Lord willing, your legacy will start a godly lineage that will reach across the future for generations to come. Yes, your name will probably be forgotten, but what you stand for will be held in high esteem for all to remember.

Perhaps you can start by documenting your family vision and mission. Write down outcomes you are praying for related to your family. Pray that your parental example of character compels your children to walk with Christ. Hold the Bible in such high regard that its commands and principles are lived out in love and obedience. Love your children with acceptance, discipline, training, and kindness. Follow the ways of God, and your children will see and secure a clear path of purpose to pursue.

Moreover, consider a family credo that defines what you value as a family. Character traits like humility, hard work, community, forgiveness, communication, and relationship. Weave these beliefs throughout the language and behavior of your family. Challenge each child to be intoxicated by Scripture, so much so that God's word is on their breath and seen through their behavior. Slow down and be intentional in legacy building. Then your children and your children's children are more apt to love Christ.

"But from everlasting to everlasting the LORD's love is with those who fear him, and his righteousness with their children's children" (Psalm 103:17).

Do I live life with legacy in mind, and do I uniquely and fully bless each child?

Related Readings: Daniel 10:19; Joshua 24:27-29; Luke 2:29; Hebrews 11:13-22

4

Gift of Grandchildren

Children's children are a crown to the aged,
and parents are the pride of their children.
Proverbs 17:6

There are privileges to maturing in age, and one of them is the gift of grandchildren. Like a king and queen's crown, they are exceptionally valuable and are to be displayed proudly. You look at their hands and feet, and you pray for them to handle life prayerfully and to walk wisely with the Lord. You gaze into their innocent eyes and see glimpses of God's glory, and you pray for them to look often to the face of Jesus and know He loves them.

Grandchildren are gifts from God that invite love and unify families. They are reminders that the Lord is at work extending His legacy. So as you love on these little ones make sure to sow into them the Word of God, and model for them grace, love, forgiveness, and fear of the Lord. Teach them to keep their eyes on Jesus, for He will never let them down. Godly grandparents invite trusting grandchildren into their lives.

Invite them to your work, so they can see how you relate to people with patience, encouragement, and accountability. Invite them into your home, so they soak in how you unconditionally love and respect their grandmother or grandfather. Make sure they catch you laughing out loud every time they visit with you. Call them on the phone; send them emails and birthday cards; take them on trips; buy them ice cream, clothes, and their first Bible. Make their memories with you bring a smile to their face.

Lastly, if you are a parent, honor your parents by allowing them to be in the presence of your children. Take a break from parenting and let your mom and dad spoil them. If you are a grandparent, be extremely grateful to your children for the opportunity to invest in their children. Honor your children by respecting their way of parenting. Work with them and not against them. Indeed, your children still need your time, money, and wisdom.

"But from everlasting to everlasting the LORD's love is with those who fear him, and his righteousness with their children's children– with those who keep his covenant and remember to obey his precepts" (Psalm 103:17-18).

How can I support my children as they parent their children?

Related Readings: Psalm 78:4-6; 128:6; Proverbs 13:22; Joel 1:2-4

5

Foolish Children

To have a fool for a son brings grief; there is no joy for the father of a fool.
Proverbs 17:21

Foolish children flail around trying to find themselves. Typically they are terrible at managing money because they have no concept of conservative spending and consistent saving. Then they look to Mom and Dad to bail them out. They desire a stimulus package from their parents, without structure or accountability. Childish children become masters of manipulation by subtly saying, "If you really loved me..." to guilt their parents into giving them what they want.

This grieves the heart of their parents. Their father and mother want to do the right thing, but become conflicted on defining what's "right." The dad may be firm and the mom more merciful, so it's imperative they are unified in their approach to how they love their rebellious child. They cannot allow Satan to drive a wedge of doubt between them. Jesus said, "... a household divided against itself will not stand" (Matthew 12:25).

Start with sincere and aggressive prayer for a loved one bound up in foolish behavior. Pray that the Lord changes you and gives you the grace and courage to offer an aggressive love based on the love of your heavenly Father. You can love the unlovely as you ought, only after receiving His unconditional love. Remember the joy you had when they came into this world as God's gift, so trust their Creator to bring them back to Christ. He can.

Lastly, confide in the Christian community about your sorrow and hurt. You may be surprised at how many have suffered a similar fate. Move beyond the mistakes of the past, and focus on faith in the present. Turn your child over to the Lord's love and discipline. Pray that your foolish child will grow fatigued from folly, and return to faith in God. Thus you pray, "Christ, give me confidence to let them go and give them to you. And I hope one day for a celebration."

"'For this son of mine was dead and is alive again; he was lost and is found.' So they began to celebrate" (Luke 15:24).

How can I best pray for and reach out to my child who is away from the Lord?

Related Readings: 2 Samuel 18:33; Proverbs 19:13-26; 2 Corinthians 2:3; 3 John 1:4

6

On Purpose

The purposes of a man's heart are deep waters,
but a man of understanding draws them out.
Proverbs 20:5

What is your unique purpose? Do you live as uniquely you, or are you fulfilling a role you really resent? Perhaps you start by asking, "What does my Savior Jesus expect of me?" Christ has clearly pronounced His purposes: "For we are God's workmanship, created in Christ Jesus to do good works, which God prepared in advance for us to do" (Ephesians 2:10). The Lord has already laid out your plan of rewarding activities on His behalf.

Start by examining your passions; not what just excites you, but the roles you are willing to suffer and persevere with on purpose. Vocational ministry may seem noble, but can you forgive in the face of rejection, and can you serve without man's recognition and affirmation? A minister's purpose is to remain a faithful servant of Jesus Christ. "And I thank Christ Jesus our Lord who has enabled me, because He counted me faithful, putting me into the ministry…"(1 Timothy 1:12). He chooses us for His purposes and glory.

Each season of life is defined by a new set of purposes. When you are single you lay a foundation of financial and moral responsibility. When you are married you prepare for a family and develop friendships with those in a similar season of life. When you have children you serve unselfishly and teach intentionally the ways of God. When you are an "empty nester" you enjoy your spouse and mentor, and aggressively invest in the Kingdom of God.

Above all, get before God and allow Him to define your purposes. Then stay on purpose with the focused disciplines of prayer and execution. If you are a teacher, teach; a student, study; a mom, mother; a dad, father; a leader, lead; If you're an artist, create; a programmer, program; a blogger, blog; a consultant, consult; a manager, manage.

Whatever you do, become the best you can be, before God and man.

"They did what your power and will had decided beforehand should happen"
(Acts 4:28).

Am I living on purpose or do I need to adjust my actions? Do my passions, gifts and skills align around a common purpose, all for God's glory?

Related Readings: Proverbs 22:6; Isaiah 46:9; Ephesians 2:11-13; Titus 2:4

7

Prime of Life

"A writing of Hezekiah king of Judah after his illness and recovery: I said, 'In the prime of my life must I go through the gates of death and be robbed of the rest of my years?'"
Isaiah 38:9-10

Your prime of life is the time for God to shine the brightest through you. He has prepared you for this purpose. It is during the prime of life that your understanding of God blossoms. Your love for people is robust. You are honest with your limitations and strengths. Your financial foundation is strong. Your family depends on God and loves you. Your experiences have caught up with your knowledge. You have become wise. Your character is Christ-like. And you still have the energy to engage with others and execute Kingdom initiatives. This has been your life preparation.

It is during the prime of your life that you can leverage the most for the Kingdom of God. Your age is between 45 and 65. The age range may vary depending on your health, maturity, and circumstances. But you have made it to this point by the grace of God. Life is all about preparation, and you have faithfully prepared. The prime of your life is a time to give it everything you've got. This is not the season to slow down for God. Rather it is time to kick it up a notch for Jesus. Crank it up for Christ. Don't hold back. Spend your influence, time, and money for Jesus' sake.

This is your prime time. Do not squander this window of opportunity. Be faithful and watch Him do miraculous works through you. Your prime of life is like participating in the Olympic Games. He doesn't prepare you for life's Olympics and expect you to coast. God's desire is for you to enjoy the "gold medal" of prayer for your intense intercession on the behalf of others at God's throne of grace. God's passion is for you to receive the "silver medal" of evangelism for your faithful sharing of the gospel. He wants to give you the "bronze medal" of discipleship for your effective teaching of the Word of God.

Indeed, there are other events for you to participate in during your prime of life. There is giving, mentoring, encouraging, rebuking, correcting, admonishing, leading, administering, mothering, fathering, grandparenting, and serving, to name a few more. Don't become idle for fear of failure. Failure is to do nothing. The Holy Spirit can better direct a moving object. Serve in the nursery at church, as an Elder, parking attendant, or greeter. Join a ministry Board of Directors. Start a ministry. Serve overseas. Prepare for your prime of life and engage in your prime of life.

"Oh, for the days when I was in my prime, when God's intimate friendship blessed my house" (Job 29:4).

Am I positioning my prime of life for the Lord's purposes?

Related Readings: Deuteronomy 1:36; Psalm 90:12; John 17:1-5

8

Faithful Fathers

The living, the living—they praise you, as I am doing today;
fathers tell their children about your faithfulness.
Isaiah 38:19

Where are the faithful fathers? Where can they be found? They can be found in church, on the little league ball fields, building sandcastles at the beach, and on their knees in prayer for their child's future spouse. They camp in the woods, buy ice cream, go shopping; teach the Bible to middle school youth and coach high school athletes. They can be found in stable societies and in cultures that love Christ. Faithful fathers matter.

Faithful fathers are not a fantasy, but a reality rooted in the fear of the Lord and care for their children. They are compelled by their heavenly Father to provide a home that nurtures, disciplines, accepts, and loves. "Fathers, do not exasperate your children; instead, bring them up in the training and instruction of the Lord" (Ephesians 6:4). They research and discover creative ways to win over their child's heart for Christ.

Faithful fathers are friends with Jesus. They see Him as a model of unselfish service, generous giving, radical responsibility, and the selflessness to put the needs of others before His own needs. "Be devoted to one another in brotherly love. Honor one another above yourselves" (Romans 12:10). Dedicated dads find strength to carry on from Christ's affirmation and accolades. They father for the audience of their heavenly Father.

Lastly, faithful fathers lead their children to know, love, and obey their heavenly Father. This is your most vital role as a dad. Children learn from your life how to live, but they need to hear from your lips how to believe. "Consequently, faith comes from hearing the message, and the message is heard through the word of Christ" (Romans 10:17). Tell them the scriptural stories of salvation, sin, forgiveness, and faith. Joseph's perseverance, Esther's courage, Moses' leadership, David's repentance, and Ruth's encouragement are examples lived by role models for them to emulate. Ask God for wisdom and grace to be a faithful father.

"After he became the father of Methuselah, Enoch walked faithfully with God 300 years and had other sons and daughters" (Genesis 5:22).

How does my heavenly Father love me? How does He want me to love my children?

Related Readings: Psalm 44:1-2; Malachi 4:6; Luke 1:7; 1 Corinthians 4:15

9

Effective Fathers Instruct

Fathers, do not exasperate your children;
instead, bring them up in the training and instruction of the Lord.
Ephesians 6:4

Men, it is not enough to just live a right life in front of your child, you must explain to them what's right. They need to know the why and the how behind what you do. Your words work wonders in their tender and teachable hearts. Your instruction means you care to coach and train them in truth. It's Dad's tutoring of his tribe that empowers his little ones for life. They may not act as if they're listening, but they are. Teaching truth transforms.

Truth leaves your lips and lodges in their heart. When you take the time to transfer truth to your child you are setting them up for success. Truth is transformational and freeing. It gives confidence, direction, and discernment. As they move into maturity you won't always be there, but truth will see them through. "Instead, speaking the truth in love, we will in all things grow up into him who is the Head, that is, Christ" (Ephesians 4:15).

Instruct them how to balance a checkbook, change a flat tire, mow the lawn, shoot a gun, dress appropriately, carry on a conversation, swim, fly a kite, book a plane ticket online, memorize poetry, journal, pray, study the Bible, grill burgers, and make homemade ice cream. Children crave being with their dad and learning his lessons from life. Tell them when you messed up, what you learned, and what you did right. Explain that their best motivations are love of God, and love for people. Teach lovingly and patiently.

Above all, teach them to know, understand, love, and fear Jesus. He is the truth. "I am the way and the truth and the life..." (John 14:6a). The more they go to Jesus, the more they will be educated in what matters most. He will reveal to them wisdom and under standing. Instruct your child in intimacy with the Almighty, and they will be inspired with a heart of humility, and they will aspire to know the mind of Christ. Lead them to sit at the feet of their Savior and learn from Him.

"Take my yoke upon you and learn from me..." (Matthew 11:29a).

How can I best instruct my child? What is their unique learning style?

Related Readings: Joshua 4:6-7; Proverbs 13:1; 1 Corinthians 2:13; 2 Timothy 3:15

10

A Delighted Parent

The father of a righteous man has great joy;
he who has a wise son delights in him.
Proverbs 23:24

Parents who love Jesus are delighted in their sons and daughters who love Jesus. There is a profound pleasure that occurs when parents can enjoy the fruit of their faithful parenting. Wise and humble parents understand that children who follow the Lord are a result of God's grace. They embrace truth because He is truth. They receive wisdom because He gives wisdom. They have discipline and understanding because they are His disciples.

Delighted parents are full of gratitude to God for the gift of godly children. Not a day goes by that they do not go to the Lord and thank Him for the love and obedience in their child's heart. It gives them great joy to see Jesus preeminent in their child's conduct and character. You honor your parents when you honor the Lord. Children, make it a goal to gladden the hearts of your parents. You are a reflection of them, so make them proud parents.

You are also Christ's representative. As a child of God, your heavenly Father delights in your heart for Him. Do people see Jesus in your attitudes and actions? Is grace and forgiveness your first response? Jesus has great joy when you worship Him in spirit and in truth. He smiles when He sees you say kind and encouraging words to hurting hearts. Your heavenly Father is also extremely pleased with your obedience to His call.

He expressed His pleasure to His Son: "And a voice from heaven said, 'This is my Son, whom I love; with him I am well pleased'" (Matthew 3:17). Do you regularly receive affirmation from the Almighty? Do you lavish affirmation on your children? Tell them how proud you are of them and their wise choices. Delighted parents do not sit silently, but celebrate Christ's influence on their offspring.

"I have no greater joy than to hear that my children are walking in the truth" (3 John 4).

Am I a delight to my Heavenly Father?

Related Readings: 1 Kings 2:1-9; Daniel 1:1-21; Luke 15:23-24; Philemon 1:9-20

11

Faithful Friendship

Perfume and incense bring joy to the heart,
and the pleasantness of one's friend springs from his earnest counsel.
Do not forsake your friend and the friend of your father.
Proverbs 27:9-10a

Faithful friendship is a relational fortress that protects you from hurt feelings and misunderstandings. When you decide beforehand to forgive and forget, there is no room for lingering resentment. Faithful friendship rises above petty arguments and selfish actions. There is a determination to push through any push backs peacefully through prayer and patience. As Jonathan said to David, "Go in peace, for we have sworn friendship with each other in the name of the LORD" (1 Samuel 20:42a).

Faithful friendships for the Christian are based on Christ. His character becomes the caliber of relationship enjoyed by both parties. You attempt to out-serve each other because Jesus served others first above Himself. Best friends forever look for ways to love without fanfare, and their expectations are an exhibition in giving, not receiving. They celebrate this transaction of double blessing. Jesus said, "It is more blessed to give than receive" (Acts 20:35b). They are a pleasant aroma that brings joy to each other's hearts.

It is good to have friends in close proximity. You enjoy their company because it is a safe and secure environment in which to be yourself. You can laugh heartily and cry unashamedly. Do you have a close confidant who gives you earnest counsel? Do you have a trusted advisor full of wisdom and discernment? Look to friends of the family who have a track record of faithfulness and wise advice. You honor your parents when you honor their friends.

Faithful friendships are a reflection of your relationship with the Lord. They are permanent, full of grace and truth.

"After Job had prayed for his friends, the LORD made him prosperous again and gave him twice as much as he had before" (Job 42:10).

Is there a faithful friendship I need to rekindle by reaching out with a phone call or visit? Whom do I need to express gratitude because of their faithful friendship all these years?

Related Readings: Ezra 10:2-5; Song of Songs 4:10; Acts 28:15; 2 Corinthians 2:15-16

12

Discernment Obeys God

He who keeps the law is a discerning son,
but a companion of gluttons disgraces his father.
Proverbs 28:7

Discernment is able to see things as they are, and determine what God expects. It's discernment that keeps college students from following the crowd into an embarrassing situation. It's discernment that allows a leader to understand the urgent need of a situation, and then call for action. It's discerning nations that comprehend the dire consequences of no common sense and loathing the Lord. "They are a nation without sense, there is no discernment in them. If only they were wise and would understand this and discern what their end will be!" (Deuteronomy 32:28-29).

Discernment is needed to protect us from others and from ourselves. For example, you may have a financial decision you are weighing as a family. Your spouse is hesitant because of the risk, and you are confident of a best-case scenario. What is the downside of waiting and taking a more conservative approach to managing cash? The check in his or her spirit may be the Lord's protection. Invite advice and you will become wiser. "A rebuke impresses a man of discernment more than a hundred lashes a fool" (Proverbs 17:10).

Remember, there are educated fools and self-educated sages. A wealthy person may be smart in the ways of the world and ignorant of the Lord, while a poor person may be ignorant by the world's standards but perceptive in God's ways. "A rich man may be wise in his own eyes, but a poor man who has discernment sees through him" (Proverbs 28:11). Do not discriminate against discerning voices from unlikely places. Strangers, enemies, and subordinates may all carry a certain amount of clarity in what's the wise thing to do.

So seek to discern God's way and obey. Like Joseph, your discernment may open doors of incredible influence. "Then Pharaoh said to Joseph, 'Since God has made all this known to you, there is no one so discerning and wise as you'" (Genesis 41:39). Discernment is a gift from God for God. It is a directive from the Spirit of God.

"The man without the Spirit does not accept the things that come from the Spirit of God, for they are foolishness to him, and he cannot understand them, because they are spiritually discerned" (1 Corinthians 2:14).

Do I prayerfully discern God's best, and then obey?

Related Readings: Psalm 119:125; Hosea 14:9; Romans 12:16; Philippians 1:10

13

Faithful Heavenly Father

A father to the fatherless, a defender of widows,
is God in his holy dwelling.
Psalm 68:5

Most people long for a faithful father who will feed them when they are hungry, love them when they are lonely, and care for them when they are crying. They long for a dad who will listen to them when they wonder, encourage them when they are discouraged, and discipline them when they do wrong. They are eager for a father who takes time for the trivial, extends wisdom in the middle of worry, and prays to understand God's will. God placed within you a desire to be loved by your father. Some fathers do well at being a faithful father and others do not. Some are extremely successful, and others fail miserably. Fortunately, God is your model of a faithful father. Your heavenly Father fills the gaps left by your earthly father; He is your faithful Father.

Your heavenly Father deserves your respect and commands your love. He says to pray, "Our Father in heaven, hallowed be your name..." (Matthew 6:9). He is a father who is totally trustworthy. You never have to doubt God's word. What He says He means, and what He means He does. Your Father in heaven will not let you down on earth. Now, sometimes it doesn't feel as if He's faithful. There are times you don't have answers for the questions that gnaw at your heart and confuse your mind. It may be that He is speaking but you are not listening. It may be that He is silent because He wants to grow your trust in Him. He will tell you what to do, in time, so while you wait, become better.

Your faithful Father in heaven is the Father of Truth. Jesus is truth (John 14:6). Satan is the father of lies (John 8:44). He acts as if he is interested in your life so he can destroy your life. He uses you for his interests. Therefore, reject the lies of the devil, and embrace the truth of the Lord. When you left the dark side of unbelief, you renounced your father, the devil, and embraced your heavenly Father through Christ. Be a lifetime learner of faithful fathering. Each season of fathering is different. What

30

worked in the last stage of your child's life needs to be adapted for the next stage.

By faith, be flexible. As infants, they need your gentle touch. As children, they need your patient instruction. As teenagers, they need your example of love and forgiveness—someone has to be the mature one (1 Corinthians 13:11). As adults, they need your wisdom and friendship. In all seasons, they need your time and trust. Above all else, look to your heavenly Father as the baseline for your behavior. Being a faithful father does not mean perfection, but it does mean you depend on the Perfect One. You lean on the Lord for His loving care, so you can extend the same. Because of your faithful heavenly Father, you can be a faithful earthly father. Invite Him to love on you and lead you into faithfulness.

How can I regularly receive the love and affirmation of my heavenly Father, so I can do the same for my children and grandchildren?

Related Readings: Matthew 5:16; 7:11; 18:10-35; John 12:28; James 1:17

14

Serve The Poor

There will always be poor people in the land. Therefore I
command you to be openhanded toward your brothers
and toward the poor and needy in your land.
Deuteronomy 15:11

What does it mean to be poor? The basic needs of food, clothing, and shelter are a struggle for the poor. Life is on hold because they are not sure from where their next meal is coming, or if what little they do eat has nutritional value. Their clothing is threadbare and insufficient to fight the elements of a blistering cold winter, or they have no home and are transient, moving from one shelter to another.

God commands us to care for the poor. However, those with abundance are tempted to judge the poor. They want to remind them that their position of disadvantage is because of poor choices. This may or may not be true, but they do not need sermonizing. What they need is to have their needs met. When we give bread to a growling stomach, we earn the right to offer the "Bread of Life" to their hungering soul. Jesus said, "I tell you the truth, he who believes has everlasting life. I am the bread of life" (John 6:47-48). Food is a friendly facilitator of conversations about Christ.

So what are some ways we can be openhanded toward the poor? Intentionality is a key to effectively reaching out to the poor. Be intentional to schedule time with them. Perhaps you engage in an after school reading program or sports activities. Your time is golden, so give some of your gold away by blocking off time to hang out with poor children.

When you wipe the nose of a child who lacks proper medicine, or, more importantly, offer the love and security of a father, you become their friend and mentor. When you talk with a single mom who is weepy because of the physical and mental abuse she has received, you become angry, and you are compelled to help her out by educating her with other options.

When a teenager is unable to have a well-balanced diet because his parents have spent the family's food money to buy drugs, your heart bleeds for them. These are the poor among you. We are insulated in our bubble of prosperity while the poor struggle in despair. Jesus walked among the poor; do I?

"Do not go over your vineyard a second time or pick up the grapes that have fallen. Leave them for the poor and the alien. I am the LORD your God" (Leviticus 19:10).

What can I do to serve just one who is poor?

Related Readings: Exodus 23:11; Leviticus 25:25; Matthew 19:21; Luke 19:8

Daily Wisdom in Your Inbox... A Free Subscription: **www.wisdomhunters.com**

33

15

Future Savings

Ants are creatures of little strength,
yet they store up their food in the summer.
Proverbs 30:25

Saving for the future is a wise way to express faith in our heavenly Father. He does His part by giving us the ability to produce resources, and He expects us to not spend it all in the present. The temptation is to take the work of our hands and have it all for now. However, it is waiting on wants and saving for needs that position us to give in our golden years. "Your beginnings will seem humble, so prosperous will your future be" (Job 8:7).

Future savings require self-denial and self-sacrifice. This is especially hard for those who are spenders. You want to reward yourself for a job well done, so you splurge and enjoy the moment. Perhaps a good process is to save 10% for long-term savings, just as you give 10% to the church and the Lord's work. Consider an automatic draft from your checking account into safe savings, so over time you adjust and don't miss the money.

Future savings give you options. Would you like to have the opportunity to take your grandchildren on mission trips or give to building orphanages around the world? Maybe. Or you may have the simple goal of access to proper healthcare. None of us want to be a burden to family or friends, but they are there to bless you.

Savings help your children to help you in your time of need. You raised them to raise you one day. "'So there is hope for your future,' declares the LORD. 'Your children will return to their own land'" (Jeremiah 31:17). Use the times you gather extra income to store up for the lean times. Just as Joseph saved grain during the prosperous days so he could provide during the days of famine.

"This food should be held in reserve for the country, to be used during the seven years of famine that will come upon Egypt, so that the country may not be ruined by the famine" (Genesis 41:36).

How can I save wisely for my family and my future needs?

Related Readings: Proverbs 21:20; 21:5 (LB); 1 Corinthians 16:2; 1 Timothy 5:8

16

Household Of Faith

Choose for yourselves this day whom you will serve...
But as for me and my household, we will serve the Lord.
Joshua 24:15

Is there enough evidence in your home for you to be convicted of following Jesus Christ? This is a choice that God gives us: a choice to center our home around faith or a facade. What happens behind the doors of your home? Is your home an incubator for faith? Indeed, your ministry begins at home. When your faith works at home, you have the credibility to export it to other environments. It is your laboratory for living.

This does not mean you are without problems, conflicts, and challenges at home. On the contrary, it is when your faith sustains you through family difficulties that it becomes a compelling reason for others to follow Christ. The question for the head of the home is, Are you the spiritual leader? As a single parent or the father or mother in the home, do you model prayer and Bible study? Does the fruit of the Spirit flow from your character? Are you involved with a community of believers in a local church?

Belief in God is a choice, so what are some wise choices you can make to build your household of faith? Begin by developing an intimate relationship with Jesus Christ. Once you are born again, you have a tremendous opportunity and responsibility to grow in your faith. Learn the Bible, apply it to your life, and let God change you from the inside out.

Next, challenge your family to do the same. Create a culture of prayer that becomes a catalyst for their time with Christ. Family devotions, small groups with other believers, and journaling are a few ways to feed the faith appetite of your loved ones. Take your family to church. This sets the stage for a week of faith and obedience.

Perhaps you read a chapter in Proverbs over dinner. Pray with your spouse. Turn off the television one night a week for thirty minutes, then discuss God's word or act out a Bible story in a play, and then pray for one another. Teach your children to pray for the sick, the lost, and the hurting. Model for them the joy of generous giving and serving.

Show them how to serve the homeless, orphans, and the elderly. Allow your kids to experience summer camps. This will galvanize their faith. It is a financial sacrifice, but it is an investment that will keep on paying dividends throughout their lives.

Talk with your family about your own struggles and failures and God's faithfulness to answer prayer and take care of you in spite of your mistakes. Your family needs to see you as much vulnerable as they see you confident. Facilitating faith in your home is a daily choice. This is one reason Jesus prayed, "Give us each day our daily bread" (Luke 11:3).

Am I a catalyst for Christ in my home? Do I serve the Lord with my family?

Related Readings: Genesis 18:19; 2 Kings 23:24; John 4:53; Acts 18:18

17

Thankful Prayers

For this reason, ever since I heard about your faith in the Lord Jesus
and your love for all the saints, I have not stopped giving thanks for you,
remembering you in my prayers.
Ephesians 1:15-16

Do you often offer a prayer of thanksgiving for the saints of God who have great faith and lavish love? Who comes to mind when you think of those who have persevered with God through pain, sorrow, joy, and abundance? Perhaps you think of career missionaries, ministers, or a successful businessperson. Maybe your mind locks onto a loved one who has kept the faith in the middle of fiery trials or a complicated health condition. These are quality human beings you can honor by thanking God for them with powerful prayers.

God expects prayer for missionaries. However, make it more personal by placing their picture in a prominent place in your home. When you walk by them or at a designated time, intercede on their behalf to Almighty God. It is those with great faith who foster a flaming fire of faith within your soul. Thanking the Lord for His faithful followers bolsters your faith to be more like those with whom you are exceedingly grateful.

Your children need to hear you pray, thanking God for the faith of your forefathers and other living family members who love Jesus. It is this attitude of respect for committed Christians that builds commitment into your sons and daughters. Gratitude to God for those who are serious about their Savior Jesus, builds a generation of God followers.

Furthermore, thank the Lord for their love. For as their faith grows, love is not far behind. "We ought always to thank God for you, brothers, and rightly so, because your faith is growing more and more, and the love every one of you has for each other is increasing" (2 Thessalonians 1:3). Those with great faith love greatly!

Pray for those with great faith and love to finish well. This is the testimony of those we admire the most. "All these people were still living by faith when they died..." (Hebrews 11:13a). Mature Christians still need encouragement and accountability to remain faithful. Your prayers for them compel them to move forward with Christ.

Whom do I know who is solid in their faith? Whom can I thank God for often in prayer? Who is a missionary couple my family can pray for weekly?

Related Readings: 2 Chronicles 30:27; Nehemiah 1:6; 1 Thessalonians 1:3; Hebrews 11:39-40

18

Grateful Children

I have no greater joy than to hear that
my children are walking in the truth.
3 John 4

Gratitude is a wonderful gift we can give to our children and our children can give to us. It brings overwhelming joy to the heart of a parent when they witness an appreciative child. "Thank you," "You're welcome," and "How can I help?" are not just polite phrases, but music to the ears of a mom and dad who long for their loved ones to grow into grateful adults.

Thankfulness is a vaccine against selfishness and discontentment. Children and teenagers who understand and apply appreciation are quick to serve others without demanding that their needs or wants be met. They take to heart what God expects of His sons and daughters: "Do nothing out of selfish ambition or vain conceit, but in humility consider others better than yourselves. Each of you should look not only to your own interests, but also to the interests of others" (Philippians 2:3-4). Gratitude leads to a Christ like attitude.

So how can you help your child learn to live a life of thanksgiving and gratitude? What does it take for a teenager to meet the needs of others before addressing their own needs? One thought is to begin teaching your child early on the value of hard work. Assign them chores and then pay them when the job is completed with excellence. Then train them to divide their money into the categories of save, give, and spend. When they invest time and energy into a meaningful outcome, they are much more appreciative of the money.

Perhaps you accompany them to feed the homeless, care for a family in financial distress, or visit those confined to jail. You may decide on a family mission trip over-seas. It may be a construction project, evangelism outreach, or loving on orphans.

Contentment and gratitude will erupt from the heart of your child when they engage people who smile in the face of ugly circumstances. They see firsthand that joy comes from Jesus, not stuff.

Therefore, be intentional about modeling appreciation in front of your offspring. Be quick to thank God and others, while slow to complain. Grateful children are attractive and pleasant to be around. Their appreciative attitude will serve them well the rest of their lives.

"Your attitude should be the same as that of Christ Jesus: Who, being in very nature God, did not consider equality with God something to be grasped, but made himself nothing, taking the very nature of a servant, being made in human likeness. And being found in appearance as a man, he humbled himself ?and became obedient to death— even death on a cross!" (Philippians 2:5-8)

How can I model an attitude of gratitude in front of my children? What can we do as a family to learn appreciation and experience contentment?

Related Readings: Deuteronomy 4:9-10; Psalm 34:11; Proverbs 22:6; Ephesians 6:4

19

Wisdom Walk

He who walks with the wise grows wise,
but a companion of fools suffers harm.
Proverbs 13:20

Who do you walk with through life—figuratively or literally—who offers you wisdom? Do you walk with your father or father-in-law, or mother or mother-in-law? When you walk with them are you slow to speak and quick to listen? Indeed, wisdom comes to those who listen more and talk less. Wisdom is a product of the people who pour their wisdom into you.

Your "wisdom walk" may be over the phone with a mentor who lives in another city, or a neighbor across the street who by God's grace has already raised grown God-fearing children. Look around you and learn from those wise ones the Lord has placed in your life. Pray for a "Paul" who can be your spiritual instructor. "Timothy, my son whom I love, who is faithful in the Lord. He will remind you of my way of life in Christ Jesus, which agrees with what I teach everywhere in every church" (1 Corinthians 4:17).

No one is ever too old or too wise to not need a regular "wisdom walk." Perhaps you take the time to walk with your spouse after dinner or a co-worker during the lunch hour. Vacations are ideal times to walk with a wise family member. Walk while the brilliant sun rises or a majestic sunset kisses the horizon. A "wisdom walk" allows your soul to catch up with the hectic pace of your body. Walk with the wise and you really will grow wise.

Talk about topics that are relevant to your season of life. Maybe it's insights into parenting a teenager, financial management, decision-making, how to love and respect your spouse, books to read, or devotion to Christ. Ask your wise walker what mistakes they made and how you can learn from them. Listen to their ideas, process them in prayer, and apply them to your life. Otherwise, unused wisdom becomes fodder for foolishness.

Above all, have wisdom walks with Almighty God. Unlike Adam and Eve, learn to live in the intimacy of the moment with your heavenly Father. "Then the man and his wife heard the sound of the LORD God as he was walking in the garden in the cool of the day, and they hid from the LORD God among the trees of the garden" (Genesis 3:8). Walk with Jesus, and you will become much the wiser. Keep Christ your closest companion.

Who are wise people in my life with whom I can enjoy regular "wisdom walks?"
What does it look like for me to have "wisdom walks" with my heavenly Father?

Related Readings: Deuteronomy 8:7; Jeremiah 7:23; Luke 6:13-17; 1 Corinthians 15:33

20

Loyalty Creates Loyalty

"But Ruth replied, 'Don't urge me to leave you or to turn back from you.
Where you go I will go, and where you stay I will stay.
Your people will be my people and your God my God. Where you die I will die,
and there I will be buried. May the Lord deal with me, be it ever so severely.
If anything but death separates you and me.'"
Ruth 1:16-17

Most people long for loyalty in love, war, and work. You can require loyalty and you may see some response, or you can show loyalty, and thus become attractive to loyalty. When you give loyalty you have a much better chance of receiving it. This is true in marriage, business, parenting, or friendship.

In marriage, how do you think unwavering loyalty makes your spouse feel? If he or she knows you are loyal to them no matter what, how will they respond? In most cases they will return loyalty, and both of you will enjoy a tremendous amount of security and peace. Adversity or difficulties should not weaken your loyalty. Rather, it should strengthen your resolve to be there for each other. Can you think of a better gift to give someone during difficult times? The quality of your relationship goes to a deeper level.

The work environment is another opportunity to exercise loyalty. A business owner or supervisor should first look at giving loyalty, rather than demanding loyalty. Will you be there for the employee during the down business cycle, as you have been when every-thing is going well? What can they expect from you? Will you be consistently honest or just when it is expedient? Wise leaders create a culture of loyalty. It means you care; it is a two way street that invites reciprocity. So, where does loyalty begin?

Loyalty begins by recognizing, understanding, and receiving God's loving loyalty. Way beyond what we have asked for or deserved, He is loyal. The Lord's loyalty overlooks my sin, my poor choices, and my pride. Like the father of the prodigal son, He is there. Even when I mope back to him embarrassed and beaten down, Jesus remains loyal.

The intensity and thoroughness of God's loyalty makes the loyalty of a Saint Bernard or a Golden Retriever look shallow. He is there to receive you back even when you are disloyal to Him. Once you recognize and understand the depth and breadth of God's loyalty to you, you can't help but extend loyalty to others. You are secure in Jesus.

You are compelled to be loyal to another because of God's great loyalty to you. How can you do otherwise? You become a loyalty maker, rather than a loyalty breaker. People trust that you are with them, that you believe in them and expect the best. You give them the benefit of the doubt. Be loyal, and there is a good chance you will receive loyalty, for loyalty creates loyalty.

Has God ever been disloyal to me? How can I remain loyal to the Lord and others?

Related Readings: Deuteronomy 31:6-8; 1 Samuel 22:14; Luke 15:11-32; Philips. 4:3

21

Surrounded By Faith

"And do not think you can say to yourselves, 'We have Abraham as our father.'
I tell you that out of these stones God can raise up children for Abraham."
Matthew 3:9

It is wise and good to be surrounded by those steeped in the faith. You are blessed if you come from a legacy of love for the Lord, a family of faith. However, do not depend on the faith of others as a substitute for your own faith. God does not have grandchildren, only children. Let your faith be inspired by the faithfulness of your righteous relatives. Make them proud of your wise choices, but avoid using them as a crutch for your convictions.

Have you been blessed with a Christian education? Are your parents in vocational ministry or highly committed volunteers in the church? If so, thank God every day for calling them to follow Christ wholeheartedly, and thank Him for their obedience. But, how do you define your faith? What do you believe about God your heavenly Father, Jesus the Savior from your sins, and the Holy Spirit, your comforter and teacher? The faithfulness of others who surround you is meant to be a steppingstone for your faith, not a surrogate.

The prayers of your parents, grandparents, and mentors are motivation for you to pray and trust God. Be careful not to allow the prayers of those who love you to be your proxy for prayer to the Lord. Indeed, familiarity in the faith can breed contempt and apathy. Once you place your faith in Christ and allow Him to cleanse your life, make sure to refill it with faithful living. Otherwise, as Jesus says, "The final condition of that man is worse than the first" (Matthew 12:45b). Fresh faith is kept alive by growing your own faith.

So how do you become a faith producer and faith reproducer? First, recognize Jesus Christ as the source of your faith. "Consequently, faith comes from hearing the message, and the message is heard through the word of Christ" (Romans 10:17). As you hear, understand and apply the word of Christ, your faith grows in grace, truth and influence.

Lastly, when you commit to teach, train, disciple, or mentor others, you are accountable to live out the truth you are transferring to other faithful followers of Jesus. As Paul told Timothy, his son in the faith, "And the things you have heard me say in the presence of many witnesses entrust to reliable men who will also be qualified to teach others" (2 Timothy 2:2). Yes, it is smart to be surrounded by faith, so you can then grow and share your own faith.

How can I better steward my legacy of faith? Who do I need to come around and encourage in the faith?

Related Readings: Genesis 12:1-3; Acts 16:29-35; 1 Corinthians 4:17; Ephesians 4:13

22

False Faith

"Not everyone who says to me, 'Lord, Lord,' will enter the kingdom of heaven,
but only he who does the will of my Father who is in heaven.
Many will say to me on that day, 'Lord, Lord, did we not prophesy in your name,
and in your name drive out demons and perform many miracles?'
Then I will tell them plainly, 'I never knew you. Away from me, you evildoers!'"
Matthew 7:21-23

There are those who claim to be Christians, but they are not. They fill the pulpits of churches, but they have not been filled with the Holy Spirit. They occupy pews, but Christ does not occupy their heart. Jesus warned that there will be those who think their religious routines will redeem them, but in the end there will be a startling revelation.

Furthermore, a person is not a believer if in one breath they claim to be a Christian, but in the next breath they deny the historical fact of His resurrection. They offer a confusing blend of belief that in the end is a rejection of the long held truths of the Church. A false faith claims Christ was a good teacher, but not a miracle worker. They deny His deity.

"And if Christ has not been raised, your faith is futile; you are still in your sins. Then those also who have fallen asleep in Christ are lost" (1 Corinthians 15:17-18).

In the last days there will be those who use religion for their own ends. So beware, and don't waste your time with counterfeit Christ followers. Their insincere efforts will only ensnare your time and money. Unfortunately, phony disciples easily dupe the weak in the faith, and when they finally wake up dazed and disillusioned, they walk away from God. So be wary of those who peddle prayer for their personal gain. Invest in the authentic.

"But know this, that in the last days perilous times will come: For men will be lovers of themselves, lovers of money, boasters, proud, blasphemers, disobedient to parents, unthankful, unholy, unloving, unforgiving, slanderers, without self-control, brutal, despisers of good, traitors, headstrong, haughty, lovers of pleasure rather than lovers of God, having a form of godliness but denying its power" (2 Timothy 3:1-5, NKJV).

Above all, secure your salvation with genuine faith in Jesus Christ, and then use your authentic influence to indoctrinate God's people in His ordinances found in the Bible. Disciple new Christians, so they are not blown away by every new attractive but bogus belief. Followers of Jesus—grounded in the truth—are able to flee from a false faith.

"Then we will no longer be infants, tossed back and forth by the waves, and blown here and there by every wind of teaching and by the cunning and craftiness of men in their deceitful scheming. Instead, speaking the truth in love, we will in all things grow up into him who is the Head, that is, Christ" (Ephesians 4:14-15).

Is my faith in Jesus Christ personal and genuine? Who can I help grow in their faith?

Related Readings: Jeremiah 14:14; 23:16; Matthew 24:24; 2 Peter 2:1

Compassion For Mother-in-laws

When Jesus came into Peter's house, he saw Peter's mother-in-law lying in bed with a fever. He touched her hand and the fever left her, and she got up and began to wait on him.
Matthew 8:14-15

Do you see your mother-in-law with compassion, or do you see her as competition? Your mother-in-law is meant to compliment your marriage, not compete with it. Peter did a smart thing as a son-in-law: he invited Jesus into his home and into their relationship. As a result, Jesus healed her so she was free to serve Him and others.

It is out of an attitude of compassion that you are able to illustrate to your mother-in-law the love of Jesus. If you resist her interest in your family, reject her suggestions, or deny her access to your home, you dishonor her in the process. Yes, we all have our quirks, but the Lord works these out with levity, love, and longsuffering. Compassion compensates.

As the leader of your home, make sure you are reaching out to your mother-in-law on a regular basis. Perhaps you invite her over for her grandchildren's birthday, school events, or sporting activities. How are you intentionally engaging your in-laws, so they are able to do life with your little ones? It is out of a multi-generational community that your offspring gain perspective from their grandparents. Honor them as models for your children, who one day will honor their own in-laws. Ruth lived this out in uncomfortable circumstances.

"Boaz replied, 'I've been told all about what you have done for your mother-in-law since the death of your husband—how you left your father and mother and your homeland and came to live with a people you did not know before'" (Ruth 2:11).

You may be concerned that your mother-in-law does not know the Lord. This is a fair fear. But it's also an opportunity for you to be a righteous representative of your Savior.

When she sees Jesus in your attitude and actions, she will be drawn by the Holy Spirit to know Him as you know Him. A fractured family is opportunity for faith to flourish.

Therefore, help facilitate faith and healing in your family dynamic by keeping Christ at the center. Ask how you can serve your mother-in-law in ways she wants to be served. Do you invite her on family outings, extended trips, or over the weekend to stay with your children? Pray your mother-in-law becomes like your mother, and you like her child.

"Greet Rufus, chosen in the Lord, and his mother, who has been a mother to me, too" (Romans 16:13).

How can I best show compassion to my mother-in-law with my attitude and actions?

Related Readings: Ruth 3:16; Micah 7:6; Luke 12:53; Ephesians 5:31

24

Trained And Mentored

"Then Paul said: 'I am a Jew, born in Tarsus of Cilicia, but brought up in this city.
Under Gamaliel I was thoroughly trained in the law of our fathers
and was just as zealous for God as any of you are today.'"

Acts 22:3

What does it mean to be trained and mentored in the ways of Jesus? Over the years, men and women invested in me by being my mentor. In one case it was a business-man who met me before sunrise. We steeped ourselves in the Scripture, and like the effects of a potent tea bag, Christ colored my heart. We prayed on our knees before the start of the day, and then stood up to walk with our Savior throughout the day. My mentor made time for me.

How can we be mentored or how can we train and mentor others? It may be a role model from a distance. However, virtual mentors have their limitations. We only see them at their best, and rarely learn how to handle struggles and disappointments. Some others have influenced us through their writings and inspired us by their insight-ful biographies.

But do you have a seasoned saint up close and personal? One who can pray with you, instruct you, challenge you, encourage you, and give you wisdom for wise decision making? "My son, pay attention to my wisdom, listen well to my words of insight, that you may maintain discretion and your lips may preserve knowledge" (Proverbs 5:1-2).

Mentors alert you to sin crouching at the door of your heart and mind. Maybe they almost lost their marriage through avoidance of responsibility or by being lured away by adultery's illusion. They can instruct you in what to do and what not to do. Paul, Moses, and David's horrific mistakes of murder did not disqualify them from mentoring and training others out of their repentant heart. Brokenness is required to mentor well.

However, it is not enough for us to just enjoy the benefits of mentoring without seeking out men and women to mentor. As Jesus commanded his mentees, "He told them, 'The harvest is plentiful, but the workers are few. Ask the Lord of the harvest, therefore, to send out workers into his harvest field'" (Luke 10:2). Then these reluctant and unproven disciples of Christ were empowered by the Holy Spirit to become workers for God. Pray to the Lord to become a mentor, and He will lead you and equip you to be an answered prayer.

"And the [instructions] which you have heard from me along with many witnesses, transmit and entrust [as a deposit] to reliable and faithful men who will be competent and qualified to teach others also" (2 Timothy 2:2, The Amplified Bible).

What profile of mentor makes sense for this season of my life? Who can I mentor?

Related Readings: Exodus 18:1-27; Judges 4:4-28; 2 Kings 2:1-15; Acts 9:26-30

25

The Spiritual Leader

But if serving the LORD seems undesirable to you, then choose for yourselves
this day whom you will serve, whether the gods your forefathers served
beyond the River, or the gods of the Amorites, in whose land you are living.
But as for me and my household, we will serve the LORD.
Joshua 24:15

What does it mean to be the spiritual leader of my home? Do I have to reach a certain level of spiritual maturity before I qualify? What if my wife is more spiritual than I am? Shouldn't she be the spiritual leader? Spiritual leadership is determined by position, not knowledge. God places a man in the role of spiritual leader to lead his wife and children in faith.

Our wife and children may know more of the Bible, but the Lord still holds us responsible for their spiritual well being. So as husbands and fathers, we have to ask ourselves, "What are we doing to lead our family spiritually?" This non-optional assignment from Almighty God forces us into faith-based behavior. We want to model daily time in Bible reading and prayer. Spiritual leaders show the way in knowing God.

"The jailer brought them into his house and set a meal before them; he was filled with joy because he had come to believe in God—he and his whole family" (Acts 16:34).

Spiritual leadership does not require a graduate degree in theology, but it does require a degree of planning and preparation. Spiritual leaders create a prayerful plan of intentional actions that expose their family to faith opportunities. You spend time looking for houses of worship that meet the needs of your wife and child, much as you would seek out the right home or school that also meet their needs. Spiritual leadership seeks out a church.

"Let us go to his dwelling place; let us worship at his footstool" (Psalm 132:7).

Men who make it a big deal to lead their family spiritually make the most difference at home and in the community. Your investment in family Bible study, your example of faith under fire, and your Christlike character are living testaments to the truth of God.

Talk about the Lord when you linger in traffic with your children, pray with them when they are fearful and upset, hold your wife's hand and listen to her heart, sign up for the next marriage retreat, and serve others unselfishly. You can't control the culture, but you and your house can serve the Lord. Spiritual leaders lead their family to love God. "For the husband is the head of the wife as Christ is the head of the church, his body, of which he is the Savior. Now as the church submits to Christ, so also wives should submit to their husbands in everything" (Ephesians 5:23-24).

How can I take responsibility to lead my family spiritually? How can I leave a legacy for the Lord?

Related Readings: 2 Samuel 12:20; Psalm 100:4; Acts 18:7; 2 Timothy 1:16

26

Affectionate Father

For you know that we dealt with each of you as a father deals with his own children,
encouraging, comforting and urging you to live lives worthy of God,
who calls you into his kingdom and glory.
1 Thessalonians 2:11-12

Am I an affectionate father? Like the geyser "Old Faithful," do I spontaneously spew out love and affection on my children? Am I faithful to fill my daughter or son's emotional tank with a warm embrace or a kiss on the head? Or am I so caught up in my own career and needs that I have no emotional capacity to give affection? Affection is displayed.

A father with affection reflects his heavenly Father's affection for him. It is out of an over-flow of being comforted and loved by Christ that redeemed fathers show affection to their children. When the Holy Spirit gives us a warm and secure hug, we can't help but hug our children and grandchildren. Eternal affection translates into earthly affection.

"Yet the LORD set his affection on your forefathers and loved them, and he chose you, their descendants, above all the nations—as it is today" (Deuteronomy 10:15).

Perhaps you have a routine of kissing and hugging your children each time you leave home and when you arrive home. There is no rushing out the door until you have made emotional deposits in your most valued relational account. Your child is your lockbox of love, waiting with a tender heart to be touched by their daddy. Initiate hugs and kisses.

When a child's heart hurts from fear, rejection, or physical harm, move closer with care and compassion. Listen with empathetic ears and outstretched arms. Affectionate fathers are up close and personal, distant fathers are unsympathetic and impersonal. Your seeds of affection reap a harvest of healthy adult children who want to come back home.

"But while he was still a long way off, his father saw him and was filled with compassion for him; he ran to his son, threw his arms around him and kissed him" (Luke 15:20b).

Since He sets His affections on you, you set your affections on Almighty God. A father who is first loved by his heavenly Father then has the capacity to love his children appropriately and fully. Adult children who have experienced their father's affection more easily show affection. So seek affection above and then apply it below.

"Let the morning bring me word of your unfailing love, for I have put my trust in you. Show me the way I should go, for to you I lift up my soul" (Psalm 143:8).

Do I regularly receive affection from my heavenly Father? How can I intentionally be the most affectionate with my children?

Related Readings: 2 Kings 17:41; Psalm 103:13; Malachi 4:6; Luke 11:13

27

Generous Dad

Which of you fathers, if your son asks for a fish, will give him a snake instead?
Or if he asks for an egg, will give him a scorpion? If you then, though you are evil,
know how to give good gifts to your children, how much more will your
Father in heaven give the Holy Spirit to those who ask him!
Luke 11:11-13

How much do I give to my children? I can give them too much money, but not too much time; I can give them too much stuff, but not too much love; I can give them too much responsibility, but not too much preparation; I can give them too much freedom, but not too much prayer. A generous dad is able to discern how much is enough for his child.

Each day, a giving father prays about the needs of his son or daughter. What does my child need from me today? What are they asking me with their words, body language, unspoken requests, or bad behavior? Extroverted children are not shy to ask for too much, while introverted children need time and space to express their needs. Treat each one according to their unique requirements. A generous dad is able to give good gifts because he understands his child. Gifts are not to compensate for our guilt, but to express our love.

For example, a good gift for a son may mean time away with dad at a sporting event or a great adventure of hunting, fishing, or hiking. However, your daughter's gift motivation may revolve around time with her dad at daddy/daughter camp, a theatrical production, or visiting the beach. Discerning dads structure good gifts around a block of quantity time.

Maybe you invest in your child with an every-other-week date night or father/son time. Ask them to pick the restaurant for dinner and/or the activity for entertainment. Your verbal and written words are a valuable gift at any age. Encourage their tender hearts, discipline their defiant hearts, affirm their humble hearts, and chide their selfish hearts. Use birthdays, graduations, proms, ballgames, auditions, and weddings to write them notes or letters of how proud you are to be their dad, and how much God loves them.

Lastly, give your offspring good gifts because of how your heavenly Father has lavished His good gifts on you. Pay forward God's gifts to you of love, patience, holiness, humility, hope, and faith. The greatest gift of salvation in Christ Jesus is meant for you to receive and give to your child. There is no greater joy than to see your flesh walking by faith.

"I have no greater joy than to hear that my children are walking in the truth" (3 John 4).

What good gift does my son or daughter need from me? How can I give them the free gift of grace?

Related Readings: Ezra 9:12; Jeremiah 32:39; Luke 10:21; Hebrews 12:7-9

28

A Faithful Father

An elder must be blameless, the husband of but one wife, a man whose children believe and are not open to the charge of being wild and disobedient.

Titus 1:6

Second only to his faithfulness to God is a father's faithfulness to his wife. His faithfulness to his children starts with faithfulness to his bride. The best gift he can give his children is fidelity in his marriage to their mom. A father's example of faithfulness breeds faithfulness in his family. The generational flow of faithfulness has a higher probability of success, because good values tend to reproduce good values.

"The LORD is slow to anger, abounding in love and forgiving sin and rebellion. Yet he does not leave the guilty unpunished; he punishes the children for the sin of the fathers to the third and fourth generation" (Numbers 14:18).

Your faithfulness to your wife sets off security in your son or daughter. Even if your wife has been unfaithful you remain faithful because your heavenly Father fuels your faithfulness. There is a higher call for a man whose heart has been captured by heaven. You do not lower your standards to what everyone else does on earth. Faithfulness remains faithful—even when a loved one is unfaithful—as this is the way of the Lord.

"The LORD said to me, 'Go, show your love to your wife again, though she is loved by another and is an adulteress. Love her as the LORD loves the Israelites, though they turn to other gods and love the sacred raisin cakes'" (Hosea 3:1).

What if I have been unfaithful? Return to God in confession and repentance. Take responsibility for your unwise decisions in the past and replace them with wise decisions in the present. Unfaithfulness from a wife or husband does reap a lifetime of consequences. However, in Christ there is healing, forgiveness, and the faith to move forward. So avoid the ugly outcomes of unfaithfulness, and remain faithful by faith.

"Who is wise? He will realize these things. Who is discerning? He will understand them. The ways of the LORD are right; the righteous walk in them, but the rebellious stumble in them" (Hosea 14:9).

Therefore, fathers go often to your heavenly Father for an infusion of integrity and perseverance. Your family, friends, and community look to you as an example of what it means to surrender to your Master, Jesus Christ. Be a faithful follower of the Lord, and your circle of influence will follow you faithfully. A father's faithfulness forges faith.

"For the LORD is good and his love endures forever; his faithfulness continues through all generations" (Psalm 100:5).

As a father, how can I be a good model of faithfulness to the Lord and my family?

Related Readings: 1 Samuel 12:24; Psalm 31:23; Proverbs 28:20; 1 Corinthians 4:17

29

A Fruitful Family

Blessed are all who fear the Lord, who walk in his ways. You will eat the fruit
of your labor; blessings and prosperity will be yours. Your wife will be like a fruitful
vine within your house; your sons will be like olive shoots around your table.
Thus is the man blessed who fears the Lord.
Psalm 128:1-4

The fruit from a family who fears the Lord is tasty and delicious. However, this type of fruit does not happen immediately, but is cultivated over time. A fruitful wife sets the tone for the home. By God's grace she weeds out criticism and replaces it with creativity. The home is her pride and joy. It is a reflection of her, as it is her nest.

A home to the wife is like an office to the husband. Things need to be just right or she feels violated. Be grateful for a conscientious wife who wants to express herself through the home. The fruit of a clean, decorated, and ordered home is calming. It provides an environment of stability, and frees family members to focus on other people and each other. A husband is free to do what he does best at work with a supportive wife at home.

A mother's influence spreads like a lovely vine throughout the house. No area is left untouched. The children are nurtured and encouraged by her sensitivity. When instilled from birth, the fruit from children become obedience to God and love for the Lord. Their heart for God grows when parents read Bible stories to them as they wait in the womb.

Family fruit flourishes when the man of the house models faithfulness. A husband's intentional effort to follow the Lord ignites faith at home. A fruitful wife has no problem submitting to a husband who submits to God. A God-fearing man is quick to confess sin to his heavenly father and to his family. It is not uncommon for him to say, "I am sorry" or "I was wrong." Authentic confession encourages confession in others.

Confessed-up hearts are family fruit. It is probable the family will pray, read their Bible, and go to church if the leader of the home does the same. Family fruit has a direct correlation to the faithfulness of the family head. Family fruit flourishes when the man fears God. Regardless of the circumstances, he is committed to doing what God expects.

Therefore, your home becomes a hot house of character. The fruit threatens to bust through the glass panels for all to see. People are encouraged when they visit your hospitable home. Sinners need a safe environment, as acceptance comes from the fruit of Christ's acceptance. Heaven's dew and rainfall keep the fruit coming to a home submitted to Christ. Jesus says, "This is to my Father's glory, that you bear much fruit, showing yourselves to be my disciples" (John 15:8). Fruit is proof of faithful families.

Does my character cultivate fruit that glorifies God in my family?

Related Readings: Genesis 7:1; Proverbs 31:15; Mark 5:19; Acts 10:2

30

Redeeming The Time

See then that you walk circumspectly, not as fools but as wise,
redeeming the time, because the days are evil. Therefore do
not be unwise, but understand what the will of the Lord is.
Ephesians 5:15-17, NKJV

What does it mean to redeem the time? It is an attitude that values every minute as a gift from God to be stewarded well. Redeeming the time trades in distrust for trust in the Lord, because He has given His children more than enough time to transact His will. It is tapping into the Lord's reservoir of wisdom and understanding in how His ways work.

For example, I can remain in a job beyond my time of full usefulness. Good things are still happening, the mission is being accomplished, but I am just biding my time. Is this the best use of God's time and resources? Maybe it's the season to transition into a situation that is a better use of everyone's time, money, and attention. Am I investing my time well?

Without being watchful of how we prioritize our time, we drift into unwise living, and miss living out the perfect will of God. It's easier to execute the expedient rather than the eternal. What does Jesus think about how you spend your time? Does it fulfill His will for you? If no, then reconsider how to better honor Christ in your career and in your choices.

What open door is before you that invites your entrance? What opportunities has the Lord given you that are waiting for your attention? By faith, walk through the open door and prayerfully plan a process to better manage your Master's opportunities. Fools complain and remain frustrated, while the wise rise to the occasion with fresh faith and fulfilling work. When you use your gifts for God the time will fly by in fruitful living for Him.

Time is short, as we are only alive a short time. We make the most of our time when we are mindful and intentional with those outside faith in Jesus Christ. Evil days engulf our life in non-eternal outcomes. So take the time to influence the lost with the message of God's redeeming love. Time is earthbound until you have a heavenly transaction of faith in Jesus. Those redeemed by God have the capacity to wisely redeem the time.

"Walk in wisdom toward those who are outside, redeeming the time. Let your speech always be with grace, seasoned with salt, that you may know how you ought to answer each one" (Colossians 4:5-6, NKJV).

Has God, through Jesus Christ, redeemed me? Am I wisely redeeming the time?

Related Readings: Deuteronomy 7:8; Psalm 78:35; Titus 2:14; 1 Peter 1:17-19

WHAT READERS ARE SAYING
ABOUT WISDOM HUNTERS

I LOVE this devotional "New Normal". I went through a divorce after 20 years of marriage. It's been three years and my 2 kids and I have moved 3 times, both kids changed schools, I changed jobs twice. I have NEVER had this much upheaval in my entire life. But… God is faithful. We are learning to live differently. We are learning to trust God irrationally. We are learning to lean on Him as the father/husband of our family. We are learning who God is in such a real way. Thanks for the encouragement! – Pam

This may be my favorite one so far. God used this to speak to me that just because we fear doesn't mean He's forgotten us. Also, He uses EVRYTHING for our good. I like how you made it personal. We need that, to see that our brothers and sisters are being real and vulnerable. Thank you. – Jacqueline

Thank you for this message of truth. A grateful follower of your online ministry. – Vivian

AMEN! I am asking God to purify my motives, and only do things for Him and His glory! Thank you this is an awesome and thought provoking devotion. God bless you! – Jenny

Wow! This message was right to the point. I asked God to reveal something that was weighing heavy on my heart, and He not only did, He surfaced it in the light. He granted the truth to me that I have been discerning in my spirit. Also to forgive myself for holding back all the hurt and forgiveness and the thing s I did or how I too behaved like a puppet on a string to please others. Thank you once again for a powerful insight and message along with the prayer of hope and scriptures to read. God bless you and your ministry. May the Lord keep blessing you with His heavenly treasures to prosper over your lives.
Love & Much Blessings Always. – Rhonda

Thank you for morning message. In the spring of this year, I received instruction from the Holy Spirit to sell my home. The instructions were exact and clear, from the realtor to be used, the price to accept, and date of closing. I followed the instructions. The house was under contract within 72 hours of listing it, for exactly the price given and the date given to close. I have been replanted in an area of the country I have never been before. After the transition period, I now find myself sitting with my heart content, feeling very complete and grateful for where I am. I know that the doors to ministry in the area will begin to open soon. There seems to be no urgency to seek or do anything but wait for Gods leading, as I know He had a reason for transplanting me, even though I do not know what His plan is. What I know is I have been and am being prepared to do Gods work exactly when I am suppose to. For now I sit, wait and rest trusting Him with my future here because God has a hope for me and a new life already planned that He is establishing. Peace be with you. Shalom. – Deborah

Once again, this was exactly what I needed! It is such a blessing to have these words at my disposal each day. especially now. We are going through such harsh financial and health trials, but our faith is daily uplifted through your website. Thank you and may God continue to bless you and your wonderful ministry. – Sondra

Thank you for what you do, the words you say, pray, and share. I have been out of work for over 4 years now and had a good solid lead on a job…today I found I was not selected….this news hurt, I felt rejected again, felt lost and wondered why God is not anwsering my prayers. I needed this message today, it spoke to my heart and made me weep. Thank you! - Becky

Also, it seems so often your words come just when I need them. Thank you for sharing. Sooo many others would hide their thoughts and words in books and keep us from hearing them and only make them available to people that can afford them. Thank you again! – Valerie

BECOMING A DISCIPLE
OF JESUS CHRIST

My journey that led me to God covered a span of 19 years, before I truly understood my need for His love and forgiveness in a personal relationship with Jesus Christ. Along this path of spiritual awakening, God placed many people along the way as spiritual guideposts directing me toward Him.

Initially it was my mother who took me to church at age 12 so I could learn about faith through the confirmation process. My grandmother was a role model in her walk with Jesus by being kind and generous to all she encountered. Once in college, I began attending church with Rita (my future wife) and her family.

It was then that relevant weekly teaching from an ancient book—the Bible—began to answer many of life's questions. It intrigued me: What is God's plan for my life? Who is Jesus Christ? What are sin, salvation, heaven and hell? How can I live an - abundant life of forgiveness, joy and love?

So, the Lord found me first with His incredible love and when I surrendered in repentance and faith in Jesus, I found Him. For two years a businessman in our church showed me how to grow in grace through Bible study, prayer, faith sharing and service to others. I still discover each day more of God's great love and His new mercies.

Below is an outline for finding God and becoming a disciple of Jesus:

1. BELIEVE: "If you declare with your mouth, "Jesus is Lord," and believe in your heart that God raised him from the dead, you will be saved" (Romans 10:9). Belief in Jesus Christ as your Savior and Lord gives you eternal life in heaven.

2. REPENT AND BE BAPTIZED: "Peter replied, 'Repent and be baptized, every one of you, in the name of Jesus Christ for the forgiveness of your sins. And you will receive the gift of the Holy Spirit'" (Acts 2:38). Repentance means you turn from your sin and publically confess Christ in baptism.

3. OBEY: "Jesus replied, 'Anyone who loves me will obey my teaching. My Father will love them, and we will come to them and make our home with them'" (John 14:23). Obedience is an indicator of our love for the Lord Jesus and His presence in our life.

4. WORSHIP, PRAYER, COMMUNITY, EVANGELISM AND STUDY: "Every day they continued to meet together in the temple courts. They broke bread in their homes and ate together with glad and sincere hearts, praising God and enjoying the favor of all the people. And the Lord added to their number daily those who were being saved" (Acts 2:46-47). Worship and prayer are our expressions of gratitude and honor to God and our dependence on His grace. Community and evangelism are our accountability to Christians and compassion for non-Christians. Study to apply the knowledge, understanding, and wisdom of God.

5. LOVE GOD: "Jesus replied: 'Love the Lord your God with all your heart and with all your soul and with all your mind.' This is the first and greatest commandment" (Matthew 22:37-38). Intimacy with the almighty God is a growing and loving relationship. We are loved by Him, so we can love others and be empowered by the Holy Spirit to obey His commands.

6. LOVE PEOPLE: "And the second is like it: 'Love your neighbor as yourself'" (Matthew 22:39). Loving people is an outflow of the love for our heavenly Father. We are able to love because He first loved us.

7. MAKE DISCIPLES: "And the things you have heard me say in the presence of many witnesses entrust to reliable people who will also be qualified to teach others" (2 Timothy 2:2). The reason we disciple others is because we are extremely grateful to God and to those who disciple us, and we want to obey Christ's last instructions before going to heaven.

Daily Wisdom in Your Inbox... A Free Subscription: www.wisdomhunters.com

MEET THE AUTHOR

Boyd Bailey

Boyd Bailey, the author of Wisdom Hunters devotionals, is the founder of Wisdom Hunters, Inc., an Atlanta-based ministry created to encourage Christians (a.k.a wisdom hunters) to *apply God's unchanging Truth in a changing world.*

By God's grace, Boyd has impacted wisdom hunters in over 86 countries across the globe through the Wisdom Hunters daily devotion, wisdomhunters.com devotional blog and devotional books.

For over 30 years Boyd Bailey has passionately pursued wisdom through his career in fulltime ministry, executive coaching, and mentoring.

Since becoming a Christian at the age of 19, Boyd begins each day as a wisdom hunter, diligently searching for Truth in scripture, and through God's grace, applying it to his life.

These raw, 'real time' reflections from his personal time with the Lord, are now impacting over 111,000 people through the Wisdom Hunters Daily Devotion email. In addition to the daily devotion, Boyd has authored nine devotional books: *Infusion*, a 90-day devotional, *Seeking Daily the Heart of God Vol I & II*, 365-day devotionals *Seeking God in the Proverbs*, a 90-day devotional and *Seeking God in the Psalms*, a 90-day devotional along with several 30-day devotional e-Books on topics such as *Wisdom for Fathers*, *Wisdom for Mothers*, *Wisdom for Graduates*, and *Wisdom for Marriage.*

In addition to Wisdom Hunters, Boyd is the co-founder and CEO of Ministry Ventures, a faith based non-profit, where he has trained and coached over 1000 ministries in the best practices of prayer, board, ministry models, administration and fundraising. Prior to Ministry Ventures, Boyd was the National Director for Crown Financial Ministries and an Associate Pastor at First Baptist Church of Atlanta. Boyd serves on numerous boards including Ministry Ventures, Wisdom Hunters, Atlanta Mission, Souly Business and Blue Print for Life.

Boyd received his Bachelor of Arts from Jacksonville State University and his Masters of Divinity from Southwestern Seminary. He and Rita, his wife of 30 plus years, live in Roswell, Georgia and are blessed with four daughters, three sons-in-law who love Jesus, two granddaughters and two grandsons. Boyd and Rita enjoy missions and investing in young couples, as well as hiking, reading, traveling, working through their bucket list, watching college football, and hanging out with their kids and grand kids when ever possible.